Dreams Really Do Come True
—It Can Happen to You!

by
Dennis Burke

Dennis Burke Publications

Dreams Really Do Come True —
It Can Happen to You!
ISBN 1-890026-08-5
© 1999 by Dennis Burke Publications
PO Box 150043
Arlington, TX 76015

Table of Contents

Chapter One

Look! The Dreamers Are Coming

There have always been men and women who refused to allow the restrictions of their surroundings to limit their faith or their dreams. These were people who seemed to stand head and shoulders above others and who would stretch their faith—and themselves to see God's plan fully come to pass.

The Bible is full of people—like Abraham, Joshua and Paul—who boldly pursued God's plan and would not relent. In the face of what seemed like impossible odds, they took God at His Word and believed Him regardless of the circumstances.

Today, the Holy Spirit has put a dream inside the heart of His family. Christians everywhere share the same longing for more of His presence, the increase of His anointing and the blessing of God on their family, business and finances. The dreamers are here now, with the dream seeds of God's abundance planted in their heart.

At a very crucial time in history, God gave two dreams to a young man named Joseph. They were dreams that would not only guide Joseph's entire life, but deliver his family and the entire nation of Israel. When Joseph began to tell others the dreams, he was misunderstood, mistreated and maligned. Yet, in spite of the mistreatment of others he kept the dreams in his heart.

One day Joseph's father, Jacob, sent him to check on the well-being of his brothers who were away tending the family flock in Shechem. Joseph had told his brothers about his dreams which caused them to develop a hatred for him that filled them with anger and rage. When they saw Joseph coming to check on them they said, "Behold, the dreamer is coming."

Joseph had told his brothers about his dream but he was no dreamer. At least not the kind of dreamer they thought he was. His dreams were powerful and filled with the seeds of his future.

Do More Than Fantasize!

Most people merely fantasize about the future. Joseph did more than fantasize—he believed his dream, he embraced his dream, he ran toward his dream, he refused to let go of his dream, and ultimately *he lived his dream!*

God is raising up people all over the world who are running toward the dreams He has placed within their hearts. They are not wasting their days wishing things were different. They have embraced the desire God has placed in them and are pursuing God to see those dreams come to life.

God has used dreamers throughout history. Jacob had a dream that would transfer the wealth of his unscrupulous father-in-law into his hands.

The Pharaoh in Joseph's time was given a dream that would show him things to come. Joseph's wisdom and insight into that dream changed the history of not only his nation, but Egypt's as well.

God used dreams to warn and guide Mary

and Joseph to protect Jesus at His birth and during His childhood. Their escape from Herod into Egypt was directed by dreams God gave to Joseph.

God-given dreams are not always given in the night. Many are like pictures of the future which He paints on the canvas of your heart. Sometimes you begin to desire specific things that actually are God-inspired desires. They can continue to increase in you, coming into focus and developing into something powerful and real on the inside. The more you realize God has shown you a part of His plan, the more empowered and directed you become.

Making God-Given Dreams Reality

There are four aspects which are important in order to see these God-given dreams become reality.

First, God will *deliver* you from all that has prevented you from receiving. John 8:31-32 says,

> Then Jesus said to those Jews who believed Him, "If you abide in My word, you are My disciples indeed. And you

10

shall know the truth, and the truth shall make you free."

When the power of God's truth is alive in your heart it makes you free. His Word does more than set you free—it makes you free! When you are made free you are a new person, free from the bondage of the past. The more God's Word is alive in your mind and spirit the more liberty you experience. You become free to think His thoughts and know His ways.

When you are free from bondage the Holy Spirit brings the Word of God to life in your inner man. As you meditate on the Word, and pray in the Holy Spirit, you experience the delivering power of God rising up within you.

In the midst of any situation, you can rely on God's strength within you to *keep* you free. When you accept Christ, you are a new person who is now free from destructive habits, thoughts and conversation. You are free to believe and act on His promises.

Each step toward God's dream for your life requires you to draw upon His strength that has been deposited in your heart. God has already given you 100 percent permanent victory. When you *know* you are totally free in Him a temporary setback will not bother you.

God's plan is to continually refine you and mold you into a more useful vessel — not through tests and trials, but through an intimate relationship with Him. Romans 2:4 tells us it's the goodness of God that leads you to repentance or change, not calamity and disaster.

The closer you walk with the Lord, the more He reveals things in your life that do not please Him. He is always teaching and encouraging you to rise up to greater levels of living. His ways are the ways that bring the greatest benefits and results in life.

David said it so well in Psalm 34:1-4:

I will praise the Lord no matter what happens. I will constantly speak of his glories and grace. I will boast of all his kindness to me. Let all who are discouraged take heart. Let us praise the Lord together and exalt His name. For I cried to Him and He answered me! He freed me from all my fears (*The Living Bible*).

In the same manner that God set David free, He has delivered you to live free from bondage.

Make God's Delight Your Delight

Second, is for God's *delight* to become your *delight*. Psalm 37:4 says, "Delight yourself also in the Lord, and He shall give you the desires of your heart."

To delight is to be soft or pliable in the Lord. It is to put His interests and priorities above your own. When you realize your own plans or pursuits are different from God's, you must choose to be soft toward Him and be changed.

Your soft and tender heart toward God becomes a powerful source of strength. When you are strong in God you become hard and intolerant of your flesh and weaknesses. This does not mean you should beat yourself up, but rather that you become strong to respond to situations according to the Word of God.

You will begin to delight to do His will. You will begin to delight to overcome your flesh and unbelief, and respond instead in obedience and faith.

13

Drawing Life Out of Your Spirit

You have been designed by God to live by the strength of your inner man. Proverbs 18:14 says,

> The strong spirit of a man sustains him in bodily pain or trouble, but a weak and broken spirit who can raise up or bear? (*The Amplified Bible*).

When you feed your spirit with the Word of God it gains strength in the same way your body becomes strong when it is fed. It is essential to feed your spirit a steady diet from the Word of God, so that when trouble comes you can draw strength from your spirit instead of reacting in the flesh.

When you allow your heart to lead your life you will find yourself peaceful and successful. It is when your flesh leads, or fear controls you that things become unbearable or out of control.

Make the decision to become soft toward God, sensitive to His leading and responsive to His directions. Then, you will abide in Him and you will get results when you pray. In John 15:7

Jesus said, "If you abide in Me, and My words abide in you, you will ask what you desire, and it shall be done for you."

To delight in God is to make His priorities yours. This becomes your key to successful prayer and effectiveness. When you delight in the Lord you can be swayed by His gentle nudge and influenced by the least little word from the Spirit of God. It is your delight to go when He says go, give when He says give or stand still when He says stand. You have become soft and pliable in His hand.

Make God's Dream Your Dream

Next, is for His *dream* to become your *dream*. A dream is bigger than you are. It is the hope of something beyond your natural reasoning. You cannot make your dreams come true without God's help.

The desires of your heart are God's dreams for you in seed form. His Word is the seed of His plans. When God's Word is hidden in your heart, doing His will becomes your inner desire and that desire will guide you directly into the center of His dream.

15

When you are honest with yourself, you can trust your inner desire and see God develop a plan to direct you into the desire of your heart. You can begin to move toward your dreams, building plans with His help and bringing those dreams to life.

Fear Keeps You From Your Dream

Fear has kept many people from living in their dream. Fear that they would not make the right decisions, fear of the unknown, fear of what others might think of them. These are all real fears, but are all based on wrong information.

Fear is faith in the wrong things. Faith believes what God has said, fear believes in the inadequacy of your own ability. Fear does not believe God's Word will work for you.

Your dreams are seeds of God's plan for your life. You are responsible to feed the dreams with faith. As you sow seeds of faith and give toward your dream, you will see it come into existence.

Many times I have known the direction God wanted me to pursue so I began to sow seeds of faith by speaking the Word of God in prayer, and by giving offerings. These acts of faith become tools in the hand of God to bring those dreams into my life.

Power Demonstrated Through You

Third, God's dreams become reality when His power is *demonstrated* through you. Everything God does *in* you He also wants to do *through* you. When you are healed, He wants to use you to bring healing to others. When you prosper, He will use you as a distributor of wealth to others.

God wants to demonstrate His power and Lordship through His Body — the Church. You are the place of His power on the earth, not because of who you are, but because you have become His dwelling place.

When you pray, your confidence is not in yourself, it is in the fact that you are in harmony with God's desire and what you ask is in accordance with His Word. When you know God's will, fear and unbelief must go. Your faith is in the power of God's Word that has the ability to bring into existence just as He has said.

First John 5:14-15 says,

> Now this is the confidence that we have
> in Him, that if we ask anything accord-
> ing to His will, He hears us. And if we
> know that He hears us, whatever we ask,
> we know that we have the petitions that
> we have asked of Him.

God will demonstrate His abundance and
victory over everything Satan has done to destroy mankind. He wants to demonstrate it
through you. When you live in the will of God
everything in your life increases.

You are called to demonstrate God's victory
over sickness and poverty. That means He wants
you healthy and abundantly supplied.

God's dream will reveal His wisdom
through His people—that's you and me. Ephe-
sians 3:10 says,

> In order that the manifold wisdom of
> God might now be made known through
> the church to the rulers and the authori-
> ties in the heavenly places (*New American
> Standard*).

God's Word is your source of strength for each step you take toward your dreams. It delivers you, stirs your desires, reveals the dreams, and empowers you to receive and demonstrate God's abundance. Abide in the Word, hide it in your heart, meditate on it and speak it in faith. You will find yourself living inside of your dreams.

Dreams really do come true — it can happen to you!

Chapter Two

Don't Let the Dream Die!

Within the heart of every believer God has deposited His ideas, plans and desires for their life. He has a beautiful course laid before each person which is waiting to be discovered.

Today, you have in your heart interests, hopes and dreams. Many of them are truly God-given. He is the One Who planted them in you like seeds. Now He expects you to unwrap them, nurture and feed them, believe and receive them. He wants His plans to become your plans and His ways to become your ways.

One of my personal favorite scriptures is found in Jeremiah 29:11 from the *New International Version,*

"For I know the plans I have for you,"

declares the Lord, "plans to prosper you and not to harm you, plans to give you hope and a future."

These hopes and dreams that God gives can be embraced, understood and cultivated. Proverbs 20:5 says, "Counsel in the heart of man is like deep water, but a man of understanding will draw it out."

Obstacles that Prevent Dreams

There can be a host of obstacles and pitfalls to seeing God-given hopes become reality.

One of the most powerful examples of this is found in the life of Joseph. As a young man, Joseph received a dream from God. He had no idea the magnitude of this dream, yet he embraced it and held on to it through some extremely trying times. He shared the dream with his brothers and found that they would become the source of one of his greatest challenges.

The dream God gave Joseph was something that would guide him toward being used to bring deliverance not only to his entire family, but his nation as well. In the beginning, his dream seemed to be more like a fantasy than reality.

Genesis 37:5-11 records the story:

Now Joseph had a dream, and he told it to his brothers; and they hated him even more.

So he said to them, 'Please hear this dream which I have dreamed:

'There we were, binding sheaves in the field. Then behold, my sheaf arose and also stood upright; and indeed your sheaves stood all around and bowed down to my sheaf.'

And his brothers said to him, 'Shall you indeed reign over us? Or shall you indeed have dominion over us?' So they hated him even more for his dreams and for his words.

Then he dreamed still another dream and told it to his brothers, and said, 'Look, I have dreamed another dream. And this time, the sun, the moon, and the eleven stars bowed down to me.'

So he told it to his father and his brothers; and his father rebuked him and said to him, 'What is this dream that you have dreamed? Shall your mother and I and your brothers indeed come to bow down to the earth before you?'

And his brothers envied him, but his father kept the matter in mind.

Joseph received these God-given dreams that revealed the deliverance God would bring to his family, the nation of Egypt and his own people, Israel. He would face a great deal of opposition that was designed to change his course and keep him from fulfilling the dreams that God had given him. But in the midst of all the opposition, Joseph kept his heart guarded and remained on track and because he did, he saw the dreams God had given him fulfilled.

When Joseph first shared his dreams with his family they ridiculed him and despised him. In fact, they hated him for his dreams and his words. How many times have believers found a promise in God's Word or realized the course

God was leading them into, and in their zeal shared this newly found truth with people close to them, only to be criticized or attacked for their faith?

It is a common mistake to believe that others will be as excited about what God is doing in your life as you are. We should be able to rejoice and have others rejoice with us. But too many times, as it was with Joseph, there is jealousy or envy over God blessing others. Rather than celebrating with you they criticize you, condemn you or even compete with you. Unfortunately, many times it is best to simply follow God's lead and say little to those around you unless you are confident they can truly be trusted.

Abusive Family Members Can't Steal Your Dream

Joseph's brothers took their hatred to the extreme and plotted how they could kill him. When Joseph's father sent him to check on the well-being of his brothers, they saw him coming and plotted his murder. Joseph's oldest brother, Reuben, convinced the others to put him in a pit and let him die there. He planned to secretly return and rescue Joseph. It wasn't that Reuben was so merciful, he was only thinking about himself. He thought he could rescue Joseph from the pit and by doing so win the favor of his father. But another brother, Judah, suggested that Joseph be sold. Soon a wandering band of Ishmaelites passed by and they sold him into slavery.

There are many today who have lived in abusive family situations but none any worse than Joseph's family. He can give you hope that all of your God-given dreams really can become reality regardless of the hardships of your past or family problems.

Integrity and Honor Bring the Blessing

Sold into slavery, Joseph served a man of considerable influence and importance in Egypt named Potiphar. There Joseph's integrity and honor for God brought the blessing of God on him and all that he set his hand to do. Potiphar saw how God favored this young man and he wisely put Joseph in a position of authority over all the business of his household.

The blessing of God came to the entire house because of Joseph and his godliness. In the face of difficulties Joseph remained faithful and true to his faith and his God.

That could become your testimony as well. Your business, your job or company can be blessed because you are there. God will honor you just as He did Joseph if you will handle yourself as he did.

What did Joseph do that brought such a powerful impact? He refused to allow bitterness or unforgiveness toward his brothers over their wickedness to influence him. Instead he chose to walk with God and bring His blessing into every situation.

Betrayal Can't Steal the Dream

Potiphar loved Joseph because of the great impact he brought into Potiphar's house. Unfortunately, Mrs. Potiphar also loved Joseph. She wanted Joseph as her own, so she pursued him. She pressured him day after day to compromise sexually. He declined and held his honor until she was so angered by his refusals that she lied and accused him of the very thing she had pressured him with.

Potiphar felt betrayed by Joseph whom he

had trusted, so Joseph was thrown into prison. Yet, even in prison the injustice did not sway him away from his standard of faithfulness. He did not complain nor compromise but held fast to the favor and blessing of God.

Even in prison God prospered Joseph until the jailer promoted him to the most trusted position in the prison. There he ministered to two men regarding dreams they each had. Joseph's interpretation to their dreams resulted in the cup bearer being restored to a position in service to the Pharaoh, and the chief baker being executed.

From Prisoner to Prime Minister

Two years later, the Pharaoh himself had a troubling dream. No one, not even the magicians nor the wise men of Egypt could tell him its meaning. The cup bearer, whom Joseph had ministered to in prison spoke to the Pharaoh about Joseph. He was immediately summoned to the Pharaoh's court.

God gave Joseph the interpretation and understanding of Pharaoh's dream. They revealed abundant harvest for seven years, followed by seven years of famine. Along with the interpretation, God gave him wisdom to know what to do.

When Pharaoh heard the wisdom of God from this young man he promoted him to the place of Prime Minister of the entire land of Egypt. From prisoner to Prime Minister in a day. Nothing is too hard for God!

The vital key that makes this story powerful is that in the midst of attack after attack Joseph refused to compromise, but remained faithful to the dream God had given him. He would not let the lies, hatred, abuse and jealousy turn him into a cynic. He kept his focus on the God he served and the dream in his heart.

Remain Faithful to the Dream

One of the most important aspects of continuing success is focus. If Satan can change your focus he can steal your strength. Jesus said in Luke 11:34,

The lamp of the body is the eye. Therefore, when your eye is good, your whole body also is full of light. But when your eye is bad, your body also is full of darkness.

The illumination and energy that light brings is produced because your eyes remain on the source of light.

Psalm 119:105 says, "Your word is a lamp to my feet and a light to my path." When you remain single-minded and focused on the Word of God that is deposited in your heart, it fills you with light that effects your entire body.

As Prime Minister, Joseph was in the position to supply the food and provisions his family needed to survive during the famine that was in the land. The dream Joseph had received was fulfilled. His entire family came to him and he became their deliverer.

Remain Faithful to Your God-Given Goal

The dreams and desires God gives you are not there to frustrate you, but rather to keep you on course for success. They can help you keep your focus even through the most difficult times.

Many people lose their way when they fail to remain faithful to their God-given goals. Far too many Christians embrace the goals that carnal people deem important or even goals that satisfy their flesh. When they do, they exchange God-given dreams for the ways of the world.

The spirit of the world says, "If it feels good, or if it's something that will impress others, it is the right thing to do." Yet, the standard of the world is never going to fulfill the dreams God places in your heart.

Those who rise up successfully and receive God's best are those who are faithful to discover God's will — then pursue it!

God is looking for nothing less than someone who will think His thoughts, pray His prayers, speak His Words and pursue the hopes and dreams He has given them until they become reality. Don't let the dream die!

Chapter Three

Attaining Your God-Given Dreams

Your inner desires are seeds—the seeds of God's dreams that drive your faith.

Every dream has a beginning and an end.

The beginning of a dream is when God places His desires and plans in someone's heart. Then, that dream becomes a reality as he or she follows God's instructions for success.

The dream that begins with a Word or promise from God will always bring uncommon results. Wisdom and common sense, coupled with the power of a promise from God, can create supernatural results.

The challenge we all face is that the steps toward success may often seem unexciting, natural or common. Ignoring the steps that may seem common or insignificant cause many people to fail to see their dreams fulfilled.

How many times have you known someone who stepped out believing that God would move for them, only to be disappointed that nothing changed? Song of Solomon 2:15 says, "Catch us the foxes, the little foxes that spoil the vines, for our vines have tender grapes." The "little foxes" are apparently insignificant things that will actually hinder the anointing of the Holy Spirit from moving freely to bring His Word to pass.

Proverbs 24:3 in *The Living Bible* brings some of the most practical and clear instruction on succeeding in our godly pursuits:

Any enterprise is built by <u>wise planning</u>, becomes strong through <u>common sense</u>, and profits wonderfully by <u>keeping abreast of the facts</u>.

In these words are answers to how to deal with a multitude of these "little foxes." God gives us three common things we can do to bring uncommon results.

Wise Planning

God is the ultimate planner! He not only planned the universe and mankind, but all of the details of your life and mine. He has a clear picture in mind of all that He desires to see accomplished in our lives. Those who see His plans and develop them will become wise planners themselves.

My wife, Vikki, is a great planner. As a co-worker in this ministry, a wife and a mother, she is what I consider a master planner. Her capacity to think ahead and develop the details of different projects or plans is really outstanding. She has developed in this aspect of the anointing and taught me a great deal by just being able to work with her.

Each year we take a motorcycle trip to various destinations across America. We ride with several couples, all of whom are ministers. Over the years Vikki has become the planner for these trips. She plans the roads we'll take, the hotels, the reservations and even some of the possible activities after we arrive.

For her, the planning is as nearly as fun and

fulfilling as the motorcycle ride itself. It is a great deal of work and responsibility, but she seems to enjoy it.

There was a time, many years ago, when she was condemned by others for her tendency to plan ahead. It sounded to some like she was not moving with the Holy Spirit or trusting God. Actually, in many ways it takes more effort and trust to plan ahead with God than to merely wait until the last minute and hope God will do something.

It is not a lack of faith to plan wisely. Yet, many people have put themselves in a position of terrible pressure because they failed to plan for their financial needs. Other people, in an effort to act in faith, have acted foolishly. They jump out of their boat hoping to "walk on the water," but they forget that Jesus only told Peter to walk on water one time. Every other time He told His disciples to use a boat.

God anoints plans when you have sought Him in the development stage. Planning leads to abundance. Proverbs 21:5 says, "The plans of the diligent lead surely to plenty, but those of everyone who is hasty, surely to poverty."

Learn to spend time planning your financial future, your family activities and your use of personal time. Wise planning is acting on your faith for the future.

In developing your plans, factor in the results of your faith and giving. Your plan will reinforce the target you have set for your faith. As you move forward in your plans, you can always review and revise them, but you will keep a clear idea of where you are and where you are going.

Common Sense

It has been said many times and it's so true: "Common sense is not common." God has given us all the ability to think and see things honestly and objectively. Common sense is acting responsibly and reasonably in light of the information you have.

As a believer, your life of faith in God's Word does not always look reasonable to others. Coming from an unbelieving perspective, they can never get a clear idea of common sense. People who are not looking to God's Word will never understand why you do many of the things you do.

On the other hand, too many believers think that common sense is contrary to acting in faith. Faith in God acts on His Word. That is common sense! But faith does not throw away acting responsibly toward the different demands you face.

For example, God's Word teaches us to honor Him through our giving of tithes and offerings. Honoring God with our substance is a vital part of our covenant life with Him. To people outside of covenant living, it does not make sense to give and expect God to bless us in our finances.

Yet, sometimes young believers have tried to impress God or others with their great faith to give. They have given in such a way that they left themselves without any money to take care of their personal responsibilities. God's Word does not tell you to "give until it hurts." That kind of giving ends up as works and not faith.

Common sense looks at the big picture and finds the wisdom of God to act in faith in every direction. Acting in faith in one area will never result in violating another aspect of obedience to God's Word.

Keeping Abreast of the Facts

Taking an honest inventory of your success and failures, your strengths and weakness, your victories and your trials, can be one of the most effective ways of assessing your spiritual progress.

To evaluate the facts as they are is the only way to clearly see the targets you need to hit. Then you can actually begin to attack the facts with the truth.

Faith in God's Word can change the facts with the power of the truth. However, if you are denying the facts exist, or you ignore the facts altogether, you lose the ability to focus your prayers and your faith. Instead, look straight at the facts that must be changed. Acknowledge the situation, then attack the facts with the truth of God's Word.

Complete honesty with yourself plays a vital role in the results you obtain.

The following are hindrances that will help you identify the things that can rob you of your focus and block the fulfillment of your God-given dreams.

Presumption

If you have embraced the Word of God, and are acting on the Word that is alive in your heart, you have every right to expect the supernatural! Real Bible faith comes from your heart, not from your mind.

You are the only one who really knows if you are ready to step out in faith on the promise of God. If you are merely hoping things work out and do not have a real assurance in your inner man, you are setting yourself up for failure.

I witnessed one young single mother as she desperately tried to get a home 'by faith' for her family. She believed God wanted to bless her, but she set her own deadline and failed to put real, faith-filled action into place. Instead, she began to talk to everyone about what God was going to do, not based on the Word, but based on her own plan. She thought she was acting in faith, but in reality she was in presumption.

The results were devastating both for her and her family. She did not receive a house by her deadline and she was embarrassed, confused and angry. She began to question everything she once believed.

You must know on the inside that you are truly acting in faith and not merely just wanting things to be different.

Harboring Unforgiveness

It is nothing new, but unforgiveness will keep you from seeing clearly, moving forward or developing godly responses. You may not have the ability in yourself, but you have the supernatural grace and ability in God to forgive the people who have wronged you.

Choosing not to forgive is to remain selfish and refuse to tap into God's grace. You will never move into the dreams and desires God has placed in your heart without letting the love of God rule your life.

Remaining Focused on the Past

Don't be a prisoner to the way you were brought up as a child. It is common for young people to shout angry words like, "I will never be like my parents!" Incredibly, when they become parents themselves, they do the same thing they despised in their parents.

Why? Because people become what they focus on. If we fail to renew our minds according to God's Word, we will revert to the training we received — even if it was wrong.

Those who will not let go of past failures and disappointments will never embrace who they are and where God is actually taking them. Their meditation on the wrong things robs them of the power to become what God declared them to be.

Set your heart to let God retrain you through His Word. You can learn new ways of thinking and acting. You can become more like your Heavenly Father than like anyone else.

A Negative Attitude

Your attitude determines your altitude. A negative attitude will keep you on the ground. People with a negative attitude always justify themselves. Proverbs 16:2 says, "All the ways of a man are pure in his own eyes, but the Lord weighs the spirits."

A negative attitude causes you to see things in life from the wrong perspective and will undermine your faith. The fear of what *could* happen will rule your thinking and steal your future.

Those with a negative attitude reflect their failure to grasp who they are in Christ, what He has already done for them and what He is doing in them now.

You can overcome a negative attitude with a daily decision to think the thoughts of God. Make the quality decision that you will not allow the limitations that negative thinking brings in your life. Fill your thoughts with the Word of God, then let the words of your mouth reflect the change in your heart.

Never justify your negative thoughts — *change them*! These are some of the hindrances that stop people in their progress. Begin now to recognize and overcome every roadblock.

Faith Will Make Dreams Come to Life

Your inner desires are the seeds of God's dreams that drive your faith. Faith will take those dreams, embrace the promise of God's

Word and make His plans come to life. Notice what Hebrews 11:6 says about faith:

> But without faith it is impossible to please Him, for he who comes to God must believe that He is, and that He is a rewarder of those who diligently seek Him.

Your reward is seeing all of God's dreams come alive in your life. It is time for you to reap the rewards that come to those who diligently seek God!

Chapter Four

Dodge the Snares
of the Dream Slayers

End times are exciting times for believers who recognize the power of God to bring to pass every promise He has spoken and every dream He has given. But for the casual or carnal Christian, these are dangerous times. In perilous times you must know the enemy's targets in order to avoid his traps. Those who are unaware may easily be caught in snares laid especially for them.

The problem is that many believers don't spot the traps because they don't understand the enemies real target. The assault against people is centered in destroying the dreams and desires God deposits in their hearts. If your enemy, Satan, can find anything to prevent you from pursuing God's plan and power, he will. And it may surprise you who and what he will use to stop you.

The Bible exposes Satan's last-days strategy in 2 Timothy 3:1-5,

> But know this, that in the last days peril-ous times will come: For men will be lov-ers of themselves, lovers of money, boasters, proud, blasphemers, disobedi-ent to parents, unthankful, unholy, un-loving, unforgiving, slanderers, without self-control, brutal, despisers of good, traitors, headstrong, haughty, lovers of pleasure rather than lovers of God, hav-ing a form of godliness but denying its power. And from such people turn away!

Notice that the dangers of these times are not the threats from obvious enemies. We are not warned here against the God haters or the world's system. The assault is from those who have a form of godliness but who deny its power. The danger we face emanates from within those who are among the people of God who have changed on the inside—people who have let their love for God grow cold.

Beware of the Dream Slayers

Think about the dream of young Joseph and what came against it. One night while Joseph slept, God implanted something deep within him that would guide and order his entire life. It was the dream of how God would raise him into a position of authority and use him.

Do you remember who it was Satan used to try to destroy that dream? The attack against Joseph's dream didn't come from enemies outside his family. It came from his own brothers.

Amazingly, these men would later be used by God to lead Israel as the fathers of the twelve tribes that formed that nation. Yet, when they first heard Joseph's dream, they were determined to destroy their younger brother though God was lifting him up. Joseph's brothers hated him, his dream and his words. Not every leader is ready to embrace God's plan when they first become aware of it.

God's Word planted in you has a very similar impact to the dream God planted in Joseph to

47

guide and order his life. God's Word revealed to you contains the plan for your future and the power to move you into every word He has spoken to you.

It's through His Word that God releases His plan and His power within you. Every word from God has enough power resident within it to fulfill itself. The battle to see God's promise destroyed or fulfilled begins the moment you receive His Word and begin to release supernatural power.

You would expect the world's point of view to be the main opposition to godly dreams. It always has and will continue to be hostile toward God. But those who must be recognized as dangerous are the ones who continue to have a form of godliness but inwardly have lost their fire. Those who once walked with God, but have now taken on the spirit of the world are the most dangerous.

Timothy's description of perilous times is the description of a society that is barren of virtue and abounding in vices—Christians who have grown cold and become unloving, unforgiving, unthankful and unspiritual. These are the real troublemakers of Christian life. They are those who have compromised their commitment to God but keep up the appearances when in your presence.

Don't be a Product of the Times

How do you steer clear of the dream slayers? As a believer, it is vital to keep yourself and develop yourself to deal with the people who are the products of the times. Second John 1:8 says, "Look to yourselves, that we do not lose those things we worked for, but that we may receive a full reward."

You need not be robbed of the full reward and increase which results from your faithfulness to God. But there is no shortcut here. You must maintain godly values and priorities and refuse to lose what has been gained.

Look again at Timothy's list of characteristics—those who have become products of their time. Of all the dangers, the most dangerous are those who have become unloving.

Can you think of anyone who had more opportunity to become unloving than Joseph? The attacks against him were painful and destructive. It would be easy to understand if he had sought a way to retaliate and pay everyone back—his brothers who sold him, Potiphar's wife who lied and had him imprisoned and even Pharaoh's butler who was blessed by Joseph yet forgot him and let him stay in prison. Years of his life seemed wasted by the betrayal of others.

Yet the life of Joseph demonstrates that with God nothing needs to be wasted. God can turn any situation around.

Love Can Turn it Around

The key to experiencing a turn around in adverse situations is maintaining the dream of God in your heart and not allowing anything to destroy it or make it ineffective.

Why is love so important? The God-kind of love is the very center of all that His kingdom is and does. God is love. So, if love is lost or compromised, every other quality of godliness is certain to be corrupted.

It was this dangerous condition in people who have walked with God that Jesus was referring to when He answered His disciples question regarding the signs of the end of time:

> And then many will be offended, will betray one another, and will hate one another. Then many false prophets will rise up and deceive many. And because lawlessness will abound, the love of many will grow cold (Matthew 24:10-12).

The word love here is the word agape, or the God-kind of love. Only those who walk with God have this love in their heart. Sadly, many will never develop the standard of love that is revealed in God's Word. Without His love as a priority in life people actually become cold in their heart.

No one starts down the path of compromise on purpose. It begins as a gradual and nearly unnoticeable decline. Once it starts, if left unchecked, the momentum can make the spiral down much easier.

Cold Love

How can the leaders in the Kingdom of God lead without lovingly touching the people they lead? How can God's family lose sight of His call to love? It happens when they choose to receive only *selective* things that God's Word says. When you *selectively receive* from God, you limit His influence in your life.

The lack of love in the Body of Christ is clearly the sign of the times. The love of many has grown cold. The evidence is everywhere — men and women of God who rightly want to touch God but selfishly neglect touching people. Others who value being right more than maintaining right relationships with others is another example of love gone cold. It is possible to do the work of God and not have the love of God in doing it.

No amount of prayer or giving will balance the scale of calloused love. Only the melting power of God's presence can replace the chill of selective love with His unconditional love.

Not a Mantelpiece — a Light

Jesus unveiled the dangerous condition of the times in a parable found in Matthew 25:1-13. There He tells of five wise and five foolish virgins who, while waiting for the bridegroom needed to keep their lamps burning bright. Of course, the five wise had enough oil, but the foolish did not. While the wise waited faithfully, the foolish left to seek a supply of oil from another place. When the bridegroom came, only the wise were there to meet him.

Of the many things Jesus was pointing to in this parable, it is easy to grasp that the lamp that lit their lives was the Word of God. Psalm 119:105 says, "Your word is a lamp to my feet and a light to my path."

The oil which made the lamps shine is the presence of the Holy Spirit Who reveals God's love to us. It is His anointing that the foolish lacked. There was no fuel to cause the lamp to shine brightly. Without love, the lamp remained only a mantelpiece.

In another place Jesus was asked about the most important commandments. In Mark 12: 30-31 is His answer:

"And you shall love the Lord your God with all your heart, with all your soul, with all your mind, and with all your strength. This is the first commandment.

53

And the second, like it, is this: You shall love your neighbor as yourself. There is no other commandment greater than these."

In all of your pursuit to grow in God, His Word and His increase, there is nothing greater than to keep your love for Him and His people burning hot. It is the most spiritual and powerful pursuit you can desire.

The God-kind of love comes out in many ways. Your words, your giving, your interest in others and even your expressions all express the love in your heart. Love is not afraid to be vulnerable to others. Love is not guarded or keeping score or wrapped up in accomplishments. Love is forgiving, kind and looking for ways of lifting others up.

Value the Dream — Not Revenge

After Joseph's father died, his brothers feared that now in his position of Prime Minister over Egypt he would retaliate against them. They sent a message to Joseph from their father begging Joseph to forgive the trespass of his brothers. In Genesis 50:17 they asked,

'Now, please, forgive the trespass of the servants of the God of your father.' And Joseph wept when they spoke to him.

What his brothers never knew about Joseph was that he had walked with God all of these years and had lived in forgiveness over the pain they caused him. He now possessed the power to repay them in the same way they treated him. He valued the relationship and the dream of God more than the sense of revenge.

Notice Genesis 50:18-21,

Then his brothers also went and fell down before his face, and they said, "Behold, we are your servants."

Joseph said to them, "Do not be afraid, for am I in the place of God? But as for you, you meant evil against me; but God meant it for good, in order to bring it about as it is this day, to save many people alive. Now therefore, do not be afraid; I will provide for you and your little ones." And he comforted them and spoke kindly to them.

He was the most powerful man on earth under Pharaoh, yet, he spoke kindly to them and comforted them. He remained tender and forgiving. His words and his actions revealed his heart.

A Place of Love, Protection and Security

In the dangerous days in which we live, the Holy Spirit is drawing us close to His presence. It is a place of love, protection and security. We have received these things freely from Him; therefore we must give freely to one another.

First Peter 1:22 admonishes believers in love toward one another,

> Since you have purified your souls in obeying the truth through the Spirit in sincere love of the brethren, love one another fervently with a pure heart.

First Timothy 1:5 echoes this truth,

> Now the purpose of the commandment is love from a pure heart, from a good conscience, and from sincere faith.

In 1 Thessalonians 3:12, Paul doesn't command you to love one another only, but he prays you increase and abound in this love,

> And may the Lord make you increase and abound in love to one another and to all, just as we do to you.

Paul admonishes the Galatians, in their call to a life of freedom to use this newly found freedom to serve one another through love.

> For you, brethren, have been called to liberty; only do not use liberty as an opportunity for the flesh, but through love serve one another (Galatians 5:13).

Finally, in 1 Corinthians 16:14 it says, "Let all that you do be done with love."

Don't let your love grow cold!

Chapter Five

Wisdom—the Master Key to Fulfilled Dreams

Remarkable results in life require rare ingredients. Pursue the one thing that can unearth the uncommon treasures of God—wisdom, the master key to fulfilled dreams.

The wisdom of God in the hands of believers is the most powerful thing on the earth. Joseph stood before the Pharaoh of Egypt filled with the wisdom of God. Though he had been confined to prison for many years, his ability to hear God's voice and receive God's wisdom remained clear.

The Pharaoh was so awed by his words that he immediately elevated Joseph out of prison and into the highest position of authority in the land under himself. Wisdom is powerful!

Possibly the greatest example of a man who operated in God's wisdom was King Solomon. Few men in history have come close to equaling Solomon's accomplishments. None have rivaled his wealth.

Wisdom Comes From God

Solomon's wisdom came from God, but the example of his father, David, gave him the heart to desire wisdom above anything else.

Shortly after David's death God spoke to Solomon through a dream. In 1 Kings 3:5 the Lord said, "Ask! What shall I give you?"

Solomon's immediate answer revealed that he knew without hesitation what was most valuable. In verse 9 he answered, "Therefore give to Your servant an understanding heart to judge Your people, that I may discern between good and evil."

Solomon was different than others. When others would ask for themselves, he asked for something that would benefit God's people and ultimately, God's plan. Most people would have asked for health, wealth or power, Solomon asked for understanding and wisdom.

Go Beyond the Ordinary

You will never rise to the top by doing the common or the ordinary. The people who see their dreams become reality go beyond the usual to the unusual, beyond the natural and into the supernatural.

It takes rare ingredients to obtain remarkable results. It takes seeking what others have not recognized as valuable to unearth the uncommon treasures of God.

Wisdom and understanding are not common. While it is available to anyone who will pursue it, there are few who have realized its value.

Solomon had seen the value of godly wisdom and understanding. He had heard the stories of his father, David, who held onto God's wisdom against all odds. He had also heard of David's departure from the wisdom of God, its devastating results and the price he paid.

Solomon's mother had also made deposits of

wisdom that set guidelines for his life. The result was that Solomon wrote proverbs that have governed for generations. His wisdom was so widely spread that kings and queens traveled great distances just to hear his words and see his wealth. The queen of Sheba was so overwhelmed by what she saw that she was breathless!

Solomon asked God for an understanding heart. God told Solomon that He would not only give him the understanding he asked for, but He would give him more than what he asked.

God gave Solomon riches, wealth and long life. God gave him all of the things he could have asked for, but did not. God wanted him healthy, wealthy and wise!

Wisdom Moves You into the Right Place

The first thing Solomon did when he woke from his dream was to leave Gibeon where he had the dream, and go to Jerusalem to stand before the ark of the covenant. The wisdom he had received from God was already working in him, and it caused him to seek the presence of God.

You will never experience a unique presence

of God if you seek Him in an ordinary way. Wisdom enters His presence in worship. The right place is in the presence of God.

The very next thing Solomon did in the presence of God was to give Him an offering. The most natural thing to do when you receive from God is to give back to God.

This spirit of giving continued to flow from Solomon toward his servants. He even blessed those who served him with a feast. Generosity will dominate the person who lives in God's presence and walks in His wisdom. Giving is the right thing in the kingdom of God.

Wisdom Opens Your Eyes to See

The wisdom of Solomon in the Proverbs is our window into the revelation which can be obtained from God. These Proverbs are intended to increase you in all aspects of life. He outlined what you could expect in chapter one, verses 2-6:

To know wisdom and instruction, to discern the sayings of understanding, to receive instruction in wise behavior, righteousness, justice and equity; to give prudence to the naive, to the youth knowledge and discretion.

> A wise man will hear and increase in learning, and a man of understanding will acquire wise counsel, to understand a proverb and a figure, the words of the wise and their riddles (*New American Standard*).

In verse 33 is one of the greatest single statements of the value of God's wisdom: "But whoever listens to me will live in safety and be at ease, without fear of harm" (*New International Version*).

The Main Ingredient for Success

Now it is easy to understand many of the other statements of wisdom and its benefits. Proverbs 4:7 says, "Wisdom is the principle thing." He did not say miracles, prayer, faith or prosperity is the principle thing. No, he said wisdom.

Wisdom is the first and foremost thing in anything you launch out to do. When God's wisdom and understanding are considered first, you are certain to avoid the snares and pitfalls which are waiting in your path. If there was more wisdom active in believers today, they would need fewer miracles!

Notice verses 11, 12 and 18 from *The Amplified Bible*:

> I have taught you in the way of skillful and godly Wisdom [which is comprehensive insight into the ways and purposes of God]; I have led you in the paths of uprightness.
>
> When you walk, your steps shall not be hampered [your path will be clear and open]; and when you run, you shall not stumble.
>
> But the path of the [uncompromisingly] just and righteous is like the light of dawn, that shines more and more (brighter and clearer) until [it reaches its full strength and glory in] the perfect day [to be prepared].

The wisdom of God in your heart will guide your steps—and even your thoughts—to rightly decide a purchase, a course of action or an approach in handling a problem. Every step you take can be a step of progress toward a godly resolution of any situation.

Success in your family, finances and any other affairs of life begins with godly wisdom that will enable you to see the real issues you face. Once you have wisdom from God, you can then approach that issue with the steps that will bring God's light on the situation.

Your path gets brighter and clearer for success and increase when you make wisdom the supreme thing.

Wisdom Finds the Plan of God

Again, Proverbs 24:3-4 in *The Living Bible* places wisdom's value in perspective:

Any enterprise is built by wise planning, becomes strong through common sense, and profits wonderfully by keeping abreast of the facts.

Wisdom from God will plan, use the knowledge available and stay informed.

Every time I go into a service to minister the

Word I have a plan. I have spent time praying and preparing and have a plan for the direction I believe God has led me. I know that the Holy Spirit may want to change the plan at the last minute because He has done it many times. Yet, more often the plan I received in my preparation was exactly the course He wanted for the service.

Too often I hear ministers say how they just want to "flow with the Spirit," therefore they fail to prepare. Usually that type of service lacks substance and the impact is minimal. For many, to "flow" only means they have lacked the discipline to prepare or wisely plan.

God is a Planner!

I've already mentioned what a great planner Vikki is, both in her spiritual and her natural life. When we strike out across the country on our motorcycle with our friends, she has plotted the course, planned the hotels and printed out a sheet of information detailing each days agenda.

Many people have in the past made her feel unspiritual for being such a planner. But one day the Holy Spirit told her that she was in good company because God had planned our entire lives before we even existed. He planned the vast universe and the systems of the earth, right down to the most intricate detail of life. *God is a planner!*

Success comes through a godly plan, using common sense and staying informed. Realize that the common sense we are talking about is not the carnal thinking some Christians maintain. For instance, it is common sense to give as the Bible teaches, but the carnal-minded Christian in many cases would disagree.

The carnal-minded person might think that you are foolish to give anything away in your situation. His thinking may sound like common sense to some, but in the kingdom of God it is foolishness.

Any time you are making a case for contradicting the Bible, you are not using common sense—you are acting like a fool! The wise will act on the Word even at the risk of looking like a fool!

I have already said that "common sense is not very common." This is even more true when you understand common sense as the wisdom found in God's Word.

Any enterprise you set out to accomplish is destined to succeed if you follow these simple, yet wise guidelines.

✳ Guidelines for Success ✳

1. *Pursue God's presence.* Worship and fellowship with the Lord and you can be confident that He will set His course for you.

2. *Give to God and honor Him.* Let His spirit of generosity begin to govern you. You will begin to look for ways to bless people and cause them to increase. Anything you make happen for someone else, God will move to make happen for you.

3. *Develop a plan with godly wisdom.* One step at a time, you will begin to see His plan become reality. Allow the Holy Spirit to lead you. He will give you thoughts and ideas that you can begin to act on. It is the doer—not the hearer only—that succeeds!

4. *If you lack the wisdom, ask God for it.* He gave wisdom to Solomon along with much more, He will give it to you too.

5. *Keep yourself informed.* Evaluate your prog-

ress. Examine your obedience to the plan God has given you. Check your heart to maintain an attitude that honors God and lifts people. Ask yourself if you are truly moving toward the dream God has placed in your heart. Then, if needed, modify your course according to the answer.

Increase is a matter of doing what God has called you to do and acting on His promises. When asked the key to his success one great leader said, "I pray, and I obey." Therein lies great wisdom.

Chapter Six

God's Dream—that We Would be Heirs of the World

God looks for men and women who will take back the things in the earth from the devil that He meant for His people to enjoy. In Christ, God has made you and I heirs of the world.

From the very beginning God had His own dream for mankind. His dream was that man would rule the earth and enjoy all that God had created for him. Man would live safe and fulfilled with God as his source and supply. And he would share in the joy of God's kingdom and walk with God daily.

God's dream has really never been altered. From the foundations of the earth, God established that each person who would ever live would be free to walk with Him and know the love of God in his or her life.

To understand God's dream is to understand the purpose of sending His Son, Jesus, into the earth. Jesus paved the way for all people to come into the family of God and inherit all of the riches of God's goodness and grace. Hebrews 1:2 tells us that Jesus has been appointed "heir of all things."

A Twofold Inheritance

As a believer, you now have an inheritance in God. That inheritance is twofold. Not only do you have the inheritance you received inwardly, but you also have the inheritance of all things. Both of these aspects — the internal and the external — are quite different from one another in nature. Yet, both are equally important to what it means to be an heir.

Think about this in terms of your natural bloodline. First, at birth you received characteristics such as the color of your eyes, the size of your nose and your height — all inherited from your family genes. These inherited characteristics helped shape who you are physically.

In the same way, as a believer, you have inherited from your heavenly Father who you are, your looks and the way you see things. It is so important that as Christians, each of us learn who we really are now that we are in God's family.

We are no longer who we once were. We are new creations in Christ, people who never existed before. We must get to know who we are and grow in our inheritance.

An Inheritance that Comes at Death

But remember, there is a second aspect of inheritance that is equally important. This is the inheritance which comes at *death*. When loved ones pass on, they leave all of the possessions that they have accumulated throughout their lives here. Those who will inherit those possessions are designated in the will of the deceased.

This same aspect exists in the inheritance that belongs to us as believers, but it has not been given the kind of attention it deserves. By Jesus' sacrifice on our behalf, He became heir of "all things." None of the *things* in this earth that He became heir of were things He needed. He redeemed it all for you and me.

But fear that they would become materialistic has caused believers to neglect this important part of what is theirs in Christ—the inheritance of things. That fear came from a wrong definition of materialism.

Materialism is not a result of having things, but of letting things take a place of priority in life. Materialism tries to fulfill emotional or spiritual needs with material things. Material things will never fill the void that only God and His Word can fill.

Repossessing the Wealth of the World

Having wealth and riches does not mean a person is materialistic any more than not having them means he or she is not.

Abraham was the first man to really walk with God and repossess the world, the land and the wealth in the world that God wanted for him. Abraham had to repossess the world because it was in the wrong hands, and God wanted it back in the dominion of people who walked with Him as He had designed in the beginning.

74

God revealed through the Apostle Paul how in Christ any man or woman could enter into the family of God and become His heir. The way was not by natural birth into the nation that began with Abraham. Instead, it was through the spiritual birth into God's family by faith.

Inheritance by Faith

Romans 4:13 sheds remarkable light on God's attitude toward this inheritance we have received:

> For the promise that he would be the heir of the world was not to Abraham or to his seed through the law, but through the righteousness of faith.

Notice Abraham and his seed would be *heirs of the world*, and this inheritance would come by faith. Abraham's example of faith would become the standard by which we can enter in. His faith was in God's Word, refusing to bow to the circumstance and conditions around him. He believed God and acted on what he believed.

You are the seed of Abraham by faith in Jesus Christ. Galatians 3:29 says, "And if you are

Christ's, then you are Abraham's seed, and heirs according to the promise."

His promise is that you, too, would inherit the world. From Abraham's day until this present time, God has looked for men and women to inherit the world and all that is in it. Psalm 24:1 says, "The earth is the Lord's, and all its fullness, the world and those who dwell therein." You are an heir of the world!

Inheritance is Now!

Jesus said it in Matthew 5:5, "Blessed are the meek, for they shall inherit the earth." Inheriting the earth is not for another age any more than meekness is. God wants His influence to reach every aspect of life *now!* He desires the assets of this earth to be transferred into the hands of holy people *now!*

This can be seen again in Psalm 37:11, "But the meek shall inherit the earth, and shall delight themselves in the abundance of peace."

The word for *inherit* means to seize, possess and even expel or cast out what does not belong. We not only receive our inheritance, but we also seize it, defend it and destroy any threat to it.

Abraham was told by God that the land where the Canaanites lived belonged to him and his descendants. He had to embrace it all by faith. The land, the descendants and the wealth would come only because he received it first in his heart.

It's Yours — Defend It!

We cannot be casual about our faith to receive. Apathy and indifference are really a slap in the face to God Who moved heaven to bring His dream to man.

Esau is an example of the danger of taking God's promises lightly. He was the firstborn son to Isaac, and Abraham's grandson. He received the birthright of the firstborn, which was very significant in their society.

Yet, it seemed unimportant to Esau. After a day of hunting, he returned home famished while his younger twin Jacob had a meal prepared for him. Jacob wanted the birthright that his brother took for granted. Jacob offered the food to Esau in exchange for his birthright, and Esau agreed to the exchange.

Indifference Toward Inheritance

Genesis 25:34 in the *New Living Translation* records this:

Then Jacob gave Esau some bread and lentil stew. Esau ate and drank and went on about his business, indifferent to the fact that he had given up his birthright.

Esau's indifference cost him everything his inheritance gave him. He failed to value the most valuable thing he possessed. He could never regain what once belonged to him.

Jacob followed in the faith of his father and grandfather. His father Isaac's faith brought him into an inheritance of land and wealth just as Abraham's faith had. Genesis 26:13 says, "He became a rich man, and his wealth only continued to grow" (*New Living Translation*).

In the same way, Jacob's faith to pursue his inheritance brought him into the dream God had for him. God spoke to Jacob and said,

I will be with you consistently until I have finished giving you everything I have promised (Genesis 28:15, *New Living Translation*).

The covenant promise God made to Abraham was working for Abraham's descendants just like God promised it would. Abraham's seed was blessed and increasing.

Receive Your Inheritance

You are now his seed and the inheritance promised to Abraham's seed is still working on your behalf! It is God's plan for each of His children to pursue Him and receive their inheritance. We are cut out of the same mold as Abraham, and God is looking to you and me to take our place and repossess His wealth in the earth today.

Isaiah declared it hundreds of years ago:

Listen to Me, you who follow after righteousness, you who seek the Lord: look to the rock from which you were hewn, and to the hole of the pit from which you were dug.

Look to Abraham your father, and to Sarah who bore you; for I called him alone, and blessed him and increased him.

For the Lord will comfort Zion, he will comfort all her waste places; he will make her wilderness like Eden, and her desert like the garden of the Lord; joy and gladness will be found in it, thanksgiving and the voice of melody (Isaiah 51:1-3).

Like Abraham, you have also been called out alone by God to bless and increase you. He will comfort you and restore all that has been wasted or destroyed. He will turn your neglected and dry places into a testimony of His power. He wants to make your life like the garden of Eden again. This time He will use you to remove the curse that sin brought and restore His dominion and abundance through you.

You Are an Heir

As His family, we are His inheritance and He is ours. Now through faith in our covenant, we take hold of the land, the wealth and the things of the earth and make them serve God as they were intended.

In your hands, the things God has created will bless you and glorify Him. According to Psalm 35:27 He takes pleasure in the prosperity of His servant. We are the family of God and heirs of the world.

God has dreamed of showing Himself strong on our behalf, and of showing Himself strong to others through us.

As you embrace God's dream and seek His ways, you will begin to experience His power to prosper—increasing everything you touch! The closer you walk with him, the more His dream will become a reality in you. You will become the living proof of Psalm 25:13. "He shall live within God's circle of blessing, and his children shall inherit the earth" (*The Living Bible*).

Chapter Seven

The Seeds of Increase
Are in Your Hands

Harvest...it's the reason for everything the successful farmer does. The plowing, the sowing, the fertilizing, the spraying is all done for the harvest. Every second of preparation and every drop of sweat is focused on one goal—to get the maximum harvest possible from the ground into which he sows.

God's Word tells us we should view life much like we observe a farmer sowing seed. We should see our part in making life productive and successful like the actions of the farmer.

The principle that the farmer uses to make his farmland productive is the same basic principle on which God's entire kingdom operates. The principle of seedtime and harvest is foundational to the working of the kingdom of God. It is the manner in which His Kingdom operates.

The importance of this great truth is clearly stated in Galatians 6:7, "A man's harvest in life will depend entirely on what he sows" (*Phillips Translation*). This means that the results you experience in life are a result of the seeds you sow.

Nothing you experience in life is exempt from this basic truth. Your present situation is largely a product of the seeds you have sown in the past. The good news is the seeds you sow today can change your future.

Your future is in your hand and in your heart in seed form. If you can learn to plant the seeds that will create the kind of life that God destined you to live in, you will find His plan becoming a reality for you.

A Law that Never Changes

This law of the Kingdom has been from the beginning. In Genesis 8:22, we see that God has declared this law will remain for all of time:

Gen 8:22

> While the earth remains, seedtime and
> harvest, cold and heat, winter and sum-
> mer, and day and night shall not cease.

Planting seeds and creating a harvest is the way God established the earth to be sustained and continue to increase. All of life is made up of sowing and reaping. If you sow the kind of seeds that will produce what you want in life, your reaping will be a joy. God's system is simple and knows no social barrier—you sow and your seeds will grow.

The person who will see increase is the one who grasps this law and develops an attitude just like the farmer. The farmer knows that reaping comes only because he sows the seeds for harvest. Second Timothy 2:6 says, "The hard-working farmer must be first to partake of the crops."

God is a God of increase. Just as He made the universe to continue to expand and the earth to continue to replenish itself, He made His entire Kingdom in heaven and on earth to bring continual increase. It's God's design! It is important to understand that God's way is to create increase.

Like the farmer in his field, you are to create

increase. And you are to be the first to benefit from the increase that comes. God expects His Word to bring increase to you. He wants you to be a source of strength and help to others. But if you have not received for yourself, it is going to be very difficult for you to help anyone else.

Participate With God's Plan

You must decide to participate in His plan for increase. He said in Psalm 115:14, "May the Lord give you increase more and more, you and your children." It is His desire that all you set your hand to will grow and be blessed.

To participate in God's plan for increase, you must understand that it does not come the way the world thinks it should. You can clearly see this exhibited in the life of Jesus.

Jesus Himself was the Seed sown to create a harvest of deliverance for all of mankind. He said in John 12:23-24

"The hour has come that the Son of Man should be glorified. Most assuredly, I say to you, unless a grain of wheat falls into

the ground and dies, it remains alone;
but if it dies, it produces much grain."

Jesus' life was to be a seed that died in the
ground, but the result would be His life multiplied in many people. He continued in verses 25
and 26 by saying,

"He who loves his life will lose it, and he
who hates his life in this world will keep
it for eternal life. If anyone serves Me, let
him follow Me; and where I am, there
My servant will be also. If anyone serves
Me, him My Father will honor."

The Way to Increase

John the Baptist said, "He must increase, but
I must decrease" (John 3:30). To the world, this
way of thinking looks upside down. That is not a
natural way of thinking, but it is the way God
works. The way up with God is first down. Increase is a result of what you give, not what you
get.

To multiply in your life, you must let go of
your own life and sow it into God's life. When
you die to yourself, you will find that His abun-

dant life will raise you to levels of living you had never imagined. Your life is now His eternal, supernatural life. The new life of God now flows within you. Philippians 2:5-11 describes this further:

> Let this mind be in you which was also in Christ Jesus, who, being in the form of God, did not consider it robbery to be equal with God but made Himself of no reputation, taking the form of a bondservant, and coming in the likeness of men.
>
> And being found in appearance as a man, He humbled Himself and became obedient to the point of death, even the death of the cross.
>
> Therefore God also has highly exalted Him and given Him the name which is above every name, that at the name of Jesus every knee should bow, of those in heaven, and those on earth, and of those under the earth, and that every tongue should confess that Jesus Christ is Lord, to the glory of God the Father.

Jesus first became as a man and let go of His

position and reputation. He did not consider His equality with God a thing to cling to but became a bondservant—a servant of love. As a result of letting go, He was given a Name that is above every name.

You do not need to fear that God is going to degrade you or crush you. He is always working to lift you and build your life into something wonderful. However, it will always mean you will have to embrace His way—letting go of the way of your flesh or reasoning. This is the way to godly increase. You sow the seeds and God brings the increase. Then you reap the harvest and enjoy the fruit. Now you have something to give others.

Living by the Fruit You Produce

Too often, people are looking to God for the wrong thing. Most people love miracles, and I do too. Yet, we are not to live for miracles. *Miracles are a result of a crisis.* When people do not live by the laws of God and a crisis comes, they have God's promise that He is on their side and wants to deliver them.

You are not limited to living from crisis to

crisis. You are to live by the fruit you produce. Remember: *Increase is a result of seedtime and harvest.*

God's Word is His will in seed form. In any area of life in which you need a harvest, you need only to plant a seed. Healing, peace, love and joy are just some of the results that are increased by sowing the seeds of God's Word.

Anything you have can become a seed that you sow. If you need love, you sow love. If you need joy, you plant joy. If you need peace, you need to be a peacemaker. The principle is clear: God has given you the tools to receive any harvest you desire — begin by planting a seed.

Your Increase is in Your Hands

One of your greatest tools for sowing and harvesting is your financial giving. Think about what money really is. It is a person's life in seed form. You give of your time and labor or ideas to gain your money. Through your money, you can sow your life into many areas of the Kingdom.

When you sow seed toward promoting the Word, you are setting increase in motion. Giving

in this way is a spiritual thing which God re-
ceives and multiplies. God can add to what you
have, however He can multiply what you give.

*When you give, your money leaves your hands,
but it never leaves your life. It leaves your present
situation, and it enters your future!*

Jesus demonstrated this one day as He was
teaching and healing a multitude of people. He
had been ministering into the evening and the
people were hungry. Notice what He did:

> When it was evening, His disciples came
> to Him, saying, "This is a deserted place,
> and the hour is already late. Send the
> multitudes away, that they may go into
> the villages and buy themselves food."
>
> But Jesus said to them, "They do not
> need to go away. You give them some-
> thing to eat." And they said to Him, "We
> have here only five loaves and two fish."
>
> He said, "Bring them here to Me." Then
> He commanded the multitudes to sit
> down on the grass. And He took the five
> loaves and the two fish, and looking up

to heaven, He blessed and broke and gave the loaves to the disciples; and the disciples gave to the multitudes.

So they all ate and were filled, and they took up twelve baskets full of the fragments that remained (Matthew 14:15-20).

Give God Something to Work With

Jesus told the disciples to take what they had and give it to Him. What they had in their hands was actually food that belonged to a young man present. Jesus blessed what the disciples gave Him and gave it back to them. But when He gave it back, there was a difference.

Once again, the disciples had in their hands the loaves and fishes, only this time it had been blessed by the Lord which supernaturally empowered it to be multiplied. The disciples began distributing the food to the people until everyone was full. They went from not having enough to having more than enough. And they did it by following one simple instruction. Jesus said, "Bring them here to Me."

If what you have in your hand doesn't meet your

need — it may be your seed!

The disciples did not have enough to meet the need, so Jesus instructed them to give what they had to Him. He has established the laws of His Kingdom to bring you into a place of abundant supply, but you must put something in His hand.

This miracle supply happened right before their eyes. That is not always the way increase comes, but increase always comes. Galatians 6:9 says, "And let us not grow weary while doing good, for in due season we shall reap if we do not lose heart."

You must not give up, but continue to sow and expect the harvest. *Due season **always** comes!*

Your increase is in your hands in seed form. Plant what you have and watch it grow!

Chapter Eight

Launch Your Attack Against Lack

The overflow of God's glory has equipped you for abundance. It has prepared you to launch an attack on your lack. Lack on any level is an enemy.

Man was not created by God to struggle with lack throughout his life. We were created to walk with God and enjoy all things. We see this in the way God took care of the first man and woman, placing Adam and Eve in a garden where every need was met. We see it in God's covenants with man—covenants He made to eventually bring man back to that place of receiving again.

Knowledge of those covenants is what caused King David to make a bold declaration in what is the most quoted passage in the Bible. In Psalm 23:1, the former shepherd said, "The Lord is my Shepherd [to feed, guide, and shield me], *I shall not lack*" (*The Amplified Bible*).

God's dream has been to bring His family back to the place of lacking nothing. Lack is at the opposite end of the spectrum from the abundance Jesus came to give us. In John 10:10 Jesus said, "I have come that they may have life, and that they may have it more abundantly."

Yes, we do face adversity and struggles. Every trial, tribulation or trouble has the potential of changing your course and leading you into faithlessness, unbelief, frustration or confusion. The way we handle those times of trouble will determine our success in coming out of lack and into abundance on every level. James 1:2-4 says,

> My brethren, count it all joy when you fall into various trials, knowing that the testing of your faith produces patience. But let patience have its perfect work, that you may be perfect and complete, lacking nothing.

In Christ, you are on a God-given course to

lacking nothing. But to continue on the road to lacking nothing, you must not be distracted by the trials that arise.

The first thing to remind yourself when any pressure rises up against you is that the joy of the Lord is your strength. Let the joy of your life in Him keep you moving toward maturity and lacking nothing. Refuse to be derailed. The closer you follow the leadership of your Shepherd, the more He will lead you out of lack on every level.

Your part in following His leadership is to walk in Bible principles that will help you attack the lack.

1. Put God and His Word First

The first vital priority toward lacking nothing is to put God and His Word first in your life. First before busyness or business. First before family, self, job or personal interests. Put Him first in all that you do, and He will direct you.

Jesus declared this priority when He settled an issue between Mary and Martha:

Now it happened as they went that He

entered a certain village; and a certain woman named Martha welcomed Him into her house. And she had a sister called Mary, who also sat at Jesus' feet and heard His word.

But Martha was distracted with much serving, and she approached Him and said, "Lord, do You not care that my sister has left me to serve alone? Therefore tell her to help me."

And Jesus answered and said to her, "Martha, Martha, you are worried and troubled about many things. But one thing is needed, and Mary has chosen that good part, which will not be taken away from her" (Luke 10:38-42).

Martha was distracted by many things. Her heart was clearly to serve the Lord, and she had invited Him into her house. Yet, her own sense of responsibility to serve kept her from the most important thing she could have done—listen to Jesus teach.

She did not see it that way. She felt that her sister Mary was being irresponsible and insensitive. She had left Martha to prepare the food and serve the people. Along with Jesus, it is likely that His twelve disciples were with Him. Martha had thirteen extra people to prepare and cook for.

This was no small task. Extra wood for the fire, extra meat, and all that was needed to serve a larger meal would take a great deal of time and effort. Martha was upset with her sister Mary for failing to do her part.

Martha was even rather pushy with Jesus, telling Him how to handle Mary: "Tell her to help me."

Martha did not yet realize that Jesus' words were more important than anything in life. She wanted to do the right thing but only knew how to serve by being busy with work.

Many times the greatest thing you can do is to sit down and let Jesus teach you in the depths of a quiet heart. Busyness does not mean you are accomplishing what God wants. Jesus did not come to Martha's house to be served food; He came to impart something. Mary was the one who had chosen to receive what He came to give.

Proverbs 3:6 in *The Living Bible* says, "In

everything you do, put God first, and he will direct you and crown your efforts with success."

Psalm 34:10 says, "The young lions lack and suffer hunger; but those who seek the Lord shall not lack any good thing."

2. Embrace the Power of Giving

The second foundation to staying on the road to lacking nothing is demonstrated in Mark chapter 10. It is the story of the rich young ruler.

This young man was hungry for more of God in his life. He ran to Jesus asking what he could do to inherit eternal life. When Jesus told him to keep the commandments, he said he had kept them from the time he was very young.

Then Jesus said something remarkable,

Then Jesus, looking at him, loved him, and said to him, "One thing you lack: Go your way, sell whatever you have and give to the poor, and you will have treasure in heaven; and come, take up the cross, and follow Me" (verse 21).

Jesus loved this man and told him to follow

Him. This young man was about to become one of the disciples of Jesus. Just one thing remained to be learned. He must learn to be a giver. He must learn the *power of giving*.

The very heart of God is in giving. John 3:16 begins, "God so loved the world that He gave...."

Giving is the central part of godly living. Jesus knew this man only needed to shift his priorities in this area and he would make a powerful disciple.

It was not that Jesus wanted this man to be poor. Poverty is a curse, and God is not bringing poverty on anyone. Jesus knew the promise of God's Word in Proverbs 19:17: "He who has pity on the poor lends to the Lord, and He will pay back what he has given." This man would have received back anything he had given. God's Word guaranteed it.

But this man walked away from Jesus sad, "But he was sad at this word, and went away sorrowful, for he had great possessions" (verse 22). He valued his possessions more than the desire in his heart for God.

When you embrace the power of giving, you

embrace God's promise of increase for all that you give. Mark 10:29-30 says,

> So Jesus answered and said, "Assured-ly, I say to you, there is no one who has left house or brothers or sisters or father or mother or wife or children or lands, for My sake and the gospel's, who shall not receive a hundredfold now in this time—houses and brothers and sisters and mothers and children and lands, with persecutions—and in the age to come, eternal life."

Even if no one has yet received one hundred fold for all of their giving, *you* can begin moving toward increase in *your* receiving. Sow into the work of His ministries and expect the power of giving to unfold for you.

3. Ask for Wisdom

Third, to continue on the road to lacking nothing will take wisdom from God. James 1:5 says, "If any of you lacks wisdom, let him ask of God, who gives to all liberally and without re-proach, and it will be given to him."

After James has referred to lacking nothing, the first thing he indicates is the need for wisdom. If you lack wisdom, ask for it.

Wisdom is insight into the real issues. It is to know the need and the answer. Wisdom gives us the ability to accurately use knowledge. The wisest man to ever write his thoughts, Solomon, said, "Wisdom is the principal thing" (Proverbs 4:7).

God will bring stability to you from His wisdom that is already in your heart. Isaiah 33:6 says,

Wisdom and knowledge will be the stability of your times, and the strength of salvation; the fear of the Lord is His treasure.

God's wisdom is available to you for the asking — wisdom for any lack you face in your marriage, finances, health or personal peace. Anything that is lacking can be brought to a place of abundance.

Jesus said He has come for this reason, "... that they may have life and enjoy life, and have it in abundance (to the full, till it overflows)" (*The Amplified Bible*).

Overflow — that is where lack comes to an end. You were made for His overflow. It is in you and available to you now. So attack your lack and let the overflow begin!

Chapter Nine

Reaping in the Days of Abundant Harvest

The harvest is crying out and the reaper is crying out. Something is about to change for those who understand the rules for reaping.

The Body of Christ is getting ready to step into the greatest aspects of reaping it has ever known. The most abundant harvest the world has ever seen is in the fields right now. It's time for us to lay claim to the "due season" to which Galatians 6:9 refers: "And let us not grow weary while doing good, for in due season we shall reap if we do not lose heart."

This is the time we can discover how to reap all that we have sown and see the multiplying impact of God's laws for harvest. It is time to put in the sickle and reap abundantly.

But first we must understand what this harvest is all about. The biblical principle of harvest primarily refers to people being born again— entering a relationship with Jesus Christ and being delivered from the power of sin. The ultimate goal of ministry is for people to know Jesus and become His disciples.

There are other aspects of harvesting that each believer must grow in personally to become a more effective part of the harvest of people for the kingdom of God. In this last-days harvest, those who reap will be those who understand the rules for reaping.

You Were Made to Reap

One of the basic conditions for reaping is that if we sow, we can reap. We sow seeds of time, love, money, spiritual truth and other things.

The problem I find is that many times people are sowing their seeds of faith through their offerings or tithes, but they are not reaping. To see the increase God has provided become a reality, we must allow the same Word that stirs us up to sow also stirs us up to reap.

We must understand how to sow in faith and reap in faith as well. God said in Proverbs 8:21 that He has given us His wisdom, "That I may cause those who love me to inherit wealth, that I may fill their treasuries."

God's desire is clear; He wants us to increase in wealth. His way to our increase is through His wisdom, and His way to wisdom is through His Word. His Word is His wisdom. By walking in it, we find the wisdom to bring wealth and increase into our lives.

Let God's Word Show You What is Yours

According to God's Word, we are to reap things which we have been defrauded from us — things withheld from our possession. James 5:1-4 gives an open rebuke to those who are rich, but whose priorities are ungodly:

> Come now, you rich, weep and howl for your miseries that are coming upon you! Your riches are corrupted, and your gar-

ments are moth-eaten. Your gold and sil-
ver are corroded, and their corrosion will
be a witness against you and will eat
your flesh like fire. You have heaped up
treasure in the last days.

Indeed the wages of the laborers who
mowed your fields, which you kept back
by fraud, cry out; and the cries of the
reapers have reached the ears of the Lord
of Sabaoth.

Notice what is crying out here. It's the wages
that are not paid. Money cries out! When you
have earned wages and are not paid those wages,
the money is still yours. Though it is not in your
hand, it cries out. It's part of your harvest.

The laws of God recognize as yours what
should have come to you but was withheld from
you. That money owed you becomes a witness
against whoever holds it wrongfully.

Part of your personal harvest is the money
and things that have been kept back from you by
the kingdom of darkness. The seed you have
sown into the Kingdom of God that has not
seemed to bring any increase is still your seed,

and the harvest remains yours. It is time to get your harvest out of the grasp of the enemy and into your hands.

If you have been defrauded, it may feel like you have been beaten. But even the courts of the land are not your final word. You have the High Court in Heaven and your Heavenly Father as the Judge. The money itself is a witness in that court. You can still win and see God restore to you anything that has been defrauded from you.

It's Time to Cry Out

Notice again in verse 4 that not only were the wages crying out, but also the reapers who had been defrauded were crying out.

If you are a sower, you are also a reaper. It is time for the reapers to cry out to receive what belongs to them. It is time for you to receive what belongs to *you*.

The Amplified Bible says that the rich "...have heaped together treasure for the last days" (James 5:3). Proverbs 13:22 says, "But the wealth of the sinner is stored up for the righteous." Wealth is made to be handled by the righteous.

I began to apply this to the sowing Vikki and I have done over the years. I realized that as diligent sowers, we are entitled to reap a harvest.

We have sown our labor, our money, our love and lives into the kingdom of God since 1971. We have seed all over the world and in many different kinds of fields. We are sowers. Yet, our reaping has not been the kind of increase our sowing could produce. We were seeing wonderful growth and increase, but not to the degree we knew was available. You remember Jesus spoke of some receiving thirty, some sixty and some a hundredfold.

Then God began to speak to me of the importance of pressing in to receive the harvest. He stirred me up to look to the fields that I had sown into and to expect a harvest in each of those fields.

Claim Your Harvest

Harvest does not come out of the field on its own. You must bring the harvest into the barns. When the reapers cry out, something different begins to happen. The seed sown, the wages withheld, the increase due begins to witness to the Father God that harvest must come into the reapers' hands.

Your enemy will steal from you and hold your goods as long as you allow. You are the one who can cry out to the Lord of the harvest and begin to reap where you have sown.

Galatians 6:7 tells us how far-reaching this sowing and reaping can go: "A man's harvest in life will depend entirely on what he sows" (*Phillips Translation*). Every aspect of life is affected by the seed you sow. You can begin to harvest in every possible area if you will sow, determine to reap and not tolerate your enemy stealing your harvest.

Power in a Decision

Some do not receive their harvest because they do not sow. You must be a sower to be a reaper. Others do not receive because they leave their increase in the field. You must put in the sickle and reap. There is power in decision. When you decide to press in and receive your harvest, there is power released through you to receive. Reaping is not automatic. Mark 4:27-29 tells how the sower sows:

111

And should sleep by night and rise by day, and the seed should sprout and grow, he himself does not know how. For the earth yields crops by itself; first the blade, then the head, after that the full grain in the head. But when the grain ripens, immediately he puts in the sickle, because the harvest has come.

You may not know how God is causing your harvest to come. He makes your seed grow, but you put in the sickle.

Lay claim to your harvest with the words of your mouth. Declare that it is yours. You have sown the seeds, and the harvest is yours for the reaping. Stir yourself up to receive it.

Seed you have sown or offerings you have given that have not seemed to bring what God's Word has promised could be held back fraudulently by your enemy. That harvest is crying out as James 5:4 states. Your seed is to bring a harvest into your hands. The harvest is made to be handled by you.

When the reaper of the harvest cries out and the harvest itself is crying out, something is about to change. To cry out to God is not to beg or complain to Him but rather to appropriate His Word and receive His promises by faith. You simply declare that His promises are true and the harvest is yours now. You decree, "I am a reaper of the promises of God."

Reap Where Others Have Labored

We are to cry out not only for what we have sown but also for what others have sown before us. Notice John 4:38: "I sent you to reap that for which you have not labored; others have labored, and you have entered into their labors."

In the covenant of increase God has made through Jesus, we are to reap beyond the seed we have sown and reap where others have labored.

What does it mean to reap where others have labored? Throughout history there have been men and women of God who have sown their offerings, their time, their families and even their own lives for the gospel. Multitudes have traveled to foreign lands to take the message of Jesus and have never seen the kind of reaping personally or in revival that their sowing should have produced.

113

They were faithful people who did not see the reality of their harvest, yet they sowed in hope and in faith. While fulfilling the dreams God had placed in their heart, they gave but did not receive in this life. Their reward in heaven is a great reward, but the seed sown in the earth has not been harvested. The enemy kept them from receiving, but their labor was not lost.

The eternal nature of spiritually sown seed continues to wait for someone to reap. The seed they have sown is still alive. Now, Jesus has sent you and me to enter by faith into their labor and reap where they have sown.

Stepping into Abundant Harvest

In Deuteronomy 6:10-11, Israel is told that God will bring them into the land He swore to Abraham, Isaac and Jacob,

> To give you large and beautiful cities which you did not build, houses full of all good things, which you did not fill, hewn-out wells which you did not dig, vineyards and olive trees which you did not plant.

Again in Joshua 24:13, God refers to this land saying,

> I have given you a land for which you did not labor, and cities which you did not build, and you dwell in them; you eat of the vineyards and olive groves which you did not plant.

The land of promise was full of blessings which they did not earn but had to pursue and receive. The picture we have of Israel entering the promise is ours also. God provided a land of milk and honey for Israel, but they had to go in and possess it.

Faith begins where the will of God is understood. Your faith can rise up above the realm you have lived in until now. You can become a reaper who is receiving more than thirty or sixty times and step into receiving more than a hundred times.

It is not time to stop or even slow down in your giving and sowing. It is time to set your faith higher and let your giving reflect the faith in your heart. Then set your heart to reap, and watch the days of abundant harvest come to you.

The People of Promise
Are Impacting Lives!

Reports come in daily from people around the world who are being changed by the power of God's Word through Dennis Burke Ministries. Reports about how God's Word has brought healing, hope, restoration to a marriage or salvation to a loved one.

Our Partners are a vital part of all the work we are doing. Every person who is changed through this ministry will have our Partners to thank. Our Partners—the *People of Promise* are those who have joined with this ministry through their monthly financial giving to help fulfill the Great Commission.

When you join in Partnership, the anointing, favor and grace that rests on this ministry will rest upon you. When you have a need in your family, your business, your finances or whatever it might be, you can draw upon the anointing that operates in this ministry to help.

Also, as a Partner you will never be without prayer! Dennis and Vikki, as well as our staff pray for you. When you send your prayer requests we join our faith with yours for the anointing of God to remove every burden and destroy every yoke!

Even though our calling is to the world, our hearts are devoted to our Partners. That's why we have designed a Collector's Series exclusively for our Partners – *People of Promise.*

The Collector's Series gives our Partners the opportunity each month to receive an exclusive teaching tape in which we teach a Word in season and pray for you.

When you send your first offering of $20.00 or more, you will receive a beautiful Collector's Series album and the first tape in the series. Each time you send your monthly offering, you can request the next tape in the series.

Join the *People of Promise* family today! Simply fill out the coupon on the following page, tear it out and enclose it with your initial partnership offering. When we receive it we will take it before God and receive you as our Partner, praying for God's best to be multiplied to you now!

Join the People of Promise Family Today!

Yes, I want to join Dennis and Vikki in fulfilling the Great Commission. Enclosed is my first offering to establish my monthly partnership.

☐ $100   ☐ $50   ☐ $20   ☐ Other _____

☐ Please send my Collector's Series album and my first tape.

Name _____

Address _____

City _____

State _____ Zip _____

Phone (_____) _____

I sow this seed in faith believing that God will meet my need:

_____

_____

Books by Dennis Burke

Develop a Winning Attitude
How's Your Love Life?
Breaking Financial Barriers
Knowing God Intimately
Grace—Power Beyond Your Ability
You Can Conquer Life's Conflicts
The Law of the Wise
*How to Meditate God's Word
The Rewards of the Diligent
A Guide to Attaining Your God-Given Goals
Yielding to the Holy Spirit

* Available in Spanish

Books by Vikki Burke

Aim Your Child Like an Arrow
Relief and Refreshing

For a complete catalog of books,
audio and video tapes or to receive
a free copy of Dennis Burke's bi-monthly
magazine, *Words to the Wise* write to:

Dennis Burke Ministries
PO Box 150043
Arlington, TX 76015

Or call toll free (800) 742-4050

Please include your prayer requests when you write.

Visit our website at:
www.dennisburkeministries.org

References

New American Standard Bible © The Lockman Foundation 1960, 1962, 1963, 1968, 1972, 1973, 1975, 1977, La Habra, California.

The Amplified Bible © The Lockman Foundation, La Habra, California, 1954, 1958.

The New Testament in Modern English (Phillips). Rev. Ed. © 1958, 1959, 1960, 1972 by J.B. Phillips. Published by Macmillan Publishing Co., New York, New York.

New Living Translation © 1996. Tyndale House Publishers, Inc., Wheaton , Illinois.

The Living Bible © 1971 by Tyndale House Publishers, Inc., Wheaton, Illinois.

New International Version © 1973, 1978, 1984 by International Bible Society.